Cerulean Wings:

The Published Works

A collection of published poems between
2014-2022

Written by:

Joseph R. Adomavicia A.K.A Joe the Poet

Contents

32. My Heart Was Given, My Will Was Not (2019)

Naugatuck Valley Community College's *"Fresh Ink Magazine"*

33. Lesson #76 (2019)

Z Publishing House's *"Connecticut's Best Emerging Poets 2019"*

34. Little Paper Hearts (2020)

Naugatuck Valley Community College's *"Fresh Ink Magazine"*

35. River Fishing (A Haiku) (2020)

Naugatuck Valley Community College's *"Fresh Ink Magazine"*

36. A Song in the Trees (Hir a Thoddaid) (2019)

Rad Press Publishing *"Cult Magazine IV"*

37. Battle Stripes (2021)

Naugatuck Valley Community College's *"Fresh Ink Magazine"*

38. Believe (2021)

Naugatuck Valley Community College's *"Fresh Ink Magazine"*

Joseph R. Adomavicia

Cerulean Wings

Even in the cold
beauty stands bold.
With leafless trees and
hints of snow covering
the limbs. And maybe
someday soon,
blue birds
will come and
sing a song,
maybe two,
with their
delightful
cerulean wings blessing
thy ears
with songs of
serenity.
Glazing thy heart
purifying,
cleansing,
from within.

On Average, America

On average,

statistics show,

students that do their

homework regularly

receive better grades

on their tests,

maybe even

live better lives.

If this is the case,

why is it that the

appointed and reappointed

leaders of America, disappoint?

No excuse for the average Joe,

if we don't take the time

to do our own homework,

govern collectively, our lives,

work together,

as we preach to our children.

Wake up America.
My mistake.
Apologize.

Pardon me, begging
words too brash,
wouldn't want to hurt
anyone's feelings now,
or would I?

On average, statistics show,
students that are regularly bullied,
their soul's stripped bare,
these children, our children,
ashamed, fearful,
so much,
they have grown unafraid
to take

Cerulean Wings

their own lives.

Laws passed, hotlines provided,
nonetheless, every day,
the innocent harassed,
the outcomes, a known forecast.

Are we not responsible,
for each and every event?

Wake up America.
My mistake.
Apologize.

School shootings,
almost weekly,
a news event that now lasts,
maybe, twenty-four hours,
do we need them to occur
daily,

before we make it they
never happen,
not once, only never.

Wake up America.
My mistake.
Apologize.

Brutish honesty,
who's got time for that,
when you can just
change the channel,
go on to the next poem?

My intent
clear.

Get apoplectic!

Intended to strike,

Cerulean Wings

the "it's ok" feelings of the
cowards who sit back,
including us,
who let these insanities
occur and reoccur.

Is that not the definition of crazy?

On average,
based on my observation,
the land of the free has been
reorganized by those,
caring for themselves,
lining their pockets with
the lazy approval,
we silent Americans
silently
permit, elect.

Let us give thanks this week,

Joseph R. Adomavicia

our lives, so far untouched,

but does not our acceptance

of all these deaths held so cheap,

dishonor our freedom,

bile our palate,

make us choke on the turkey?

Has our notion of freedom,

become so self-centered,

diminished, tarnished,

even corrupted?

America, on average,

we cannot be

who we want to be,

a "United State,"

if we are content to be on average.

We Americans Refacing the Nation

Think of our country

as one big puzzle.

Each piece fits snug

into but one or two others,

there is no

great art in that.

Are we but

a small pretense?

Artfully pretending

that we are all

just one poem,

same puzzle.

Those who would

categorize, segregate,

instinctually face-divide.

Can a face fully function when

parted by color, faith,
puzzle pieces, eyes, ears, cut off,
insular, singular, dissected entities,
a solitary piece,
a completed poem be?

It cannot be so.

The different pieces,
individual unique shaped.
Yet, as a babe to old man,
the face the same, yet
ever changing,
the only constancy,
the change of change.

Refacing the nation.

There are pseudo-trigger pullers.
Dividers, our politicians.
Lawyers, who sue for the

profits of division,
not for Justice.
We are the electors
of those who proclaim
bigotry
in our name.

So let us segregate ourselves,
in Unity,
let us categorize ourselves,
as
we, Americans,
one nation that never ceases to
reface for the better.

Joseph R. Adomavicia

The Very Best and Very Worst

If only I were to meet

a woman

who spoke to me

in all her intensities

I would embrace

her propensity passionately

and cherish

the inferno writhing

from the deepest crevices

of her soul—

at least then

I would be able to understand

the very worst

and very best of her.

Have You Ever?

I wonder—

have you ever taken the time to notice,

how summer's sun

can clear gunmetal skies,

or how it refracts off the water

of somber heaven—

filling the darkness behind your eyes?

I wonder—

have you ever taken the time to notice,

how when spring's roses

begin to blossom

the wind carries love's scent

through the air

or how it effortlessly enraptures—

permeating beauty

from within the pigment of its petals?

Joseph R. Adomavicia

I wonder—

have you ever taken the time to notice,

how the cycle of autumn's leaves

remains parallel

to the frailty of the living

or how the perpetuity of their purpose

is either known of and ignored or

understood and accepted?

I wonder—

have you ever taken the time to notice,

how the winter's deep freeze

blankets and preserves the earth

beneath our feet

to walk upon in new years to come,

or how it brings forth the warmth of

family's serenity?

Beyond the Clouds

It looked like heaven was

just beyond the clouds,

lucid voices from afar spoke words

of tarnished beauty.

Bearing an aura,

drawing me close,

offering comfort and solace

as a keepsake of the imminent.

Where my faith lies,

I am unsure—

and here I stand searching

for meaning unsure of the cause.

Joseph R. Adomavicia

Half-Mast

The American flag spends another day
hanging at half-mast.
Its people are in distress,
and the blood flow of commonality
is imbued into the city streets.
The lives of innocence and of family's
mothers and fathers,
sons and daughters,
brothers and sisters,
nieces and nephews
all derived of the same human element,
all coexisting in the same planet,
only in different locations,
yet these same individuals are
slaughtered for the prevalence
of particular causes and beliefs
of an individual group.
Whether the cause is for
religion or money,

Cerulean Wings

whether the outcome is in result

of psychological disorder,

or the old tale of revenge,

no matter which way you cut it

killing is killing, murder is murder.

Is there truly a just cause to kill?

Is peace on earth just a naïve notion?

Something never to exist

until there is not one human that exists?

For the sake of the human race,

for the sake of our world,

and our children yet to come,

I hope this notion of new-found peace

perceived to be inconceivable,

is the reason the American flag

once again, rises from half-mast.

Joseph R. Adomavicia

The Trinity of a Stressful Life

What to do, what to do,
but wake up, earn a buck,
wash up, sleep, and repeat.
It's the same ole' stress wearing me
down—
down to the bone.
Have to earn more money
for the better of a company
that simple doesn't give a damn.
Can't stop working now though,
no retiring for me,
there is food to put on the table,
there are bills, and taxes to pay—
another blue-collared worker
working their week away.

What to do, what to do,
but wake up, earn a buck,
wash up, sleep, and repeat.

Cerulean Wings

It's the same ole' stress wearing me
down—
down to the bone.
Fellow citizen,
do we pledge allegiance
to one another for which we stand?
Or do we just make claims,
assumptions, and accusations,
yet our faces, our cases, our intuition,
our missions, our grief, our beliefs,
are visions seen through a narrow scope.
United we stand or divided we fall.
Will we let one another fall?
Will we redefine hypocrisy?
Or shall we become the epitome of unity?

What to do, what to do,
but wake up, earn a buck,
wash up, sleep, and repeat.

Joseph R. Adomavicia

It's the same ole' stress wearing me
down—
down to the bone.
We all have set goals, dreamt
and felt contempt if we fell short,
but at the end of the day
do we ever question why this is?
Do we even consider how bitter
life would be if we continuously
hold ourselves back?
I say it is either love or the lack thereof.
We are either foolishly complacent,
or dangerously discontent.
Take control of mind, soul, and spirit.
Refuse to eat the bullet,
and don't ever be the lone voice of
complaints,
for, a voice that bickers will be forgotten
that much quicker.

The Root of All Evil

If money is the root of all evil,

then what about the people

that use it daily?

If guns are the root of all

senseless shootings,

then what about the individuals behind

the guns being used?

If religion is meant to be a source of faith

in concurrence

of what is and what was holy,

then what about the wars caused by the

difference of religion?

If politics are to govern,

create order, and exact justice,

then what about the politicians

who run it,

ruining the principles of justice and law

before conception even occurs?

Joseph R. Adomavicia

If Mother Nature is the cause of the

Earth's natural disasters,

then what about the peoples' careless

pollution of the planet?

And that's just it,

people

have polluted the world

yet, deem everything else evil

except for the darkness

that resides in the hearts of many.

Is This the Mercy We've Prayed For?

Wiry wrath has crawled through this world.

A silver lining in the sky

like a spider's web in sunlight.

Is this the mercy we've prayed for?

Does the guilt lie in the web's entrapment

or does it linger in its captives?

Is this simply karma giving us

what we as a collective

have given to the world, just in return?

Have we a chance to break free from

these webs of torment,

these webs that hold us back,

if we continue to fight one another

in the process?

I ask again,

is this the mercy we've prayed for?

Joseph R. Adomavicia

Web Weaving (A Haiku)

We weave webs where we

want Why wander wayward where

whirlwinds whip wildly

The Raven and the Dove

As I've walked through life,

the raven has always flown closer

than the dove.

It's intentions to manipulate the

peace the uncaged dove nourishes with.

It's motive grim like the reaper's scythe.

It lurks, dipping in and out of

venues of darkness

darting towards its prey.

But no matter, it's cannibalistic

bloodthirsty mentality

shrivels into nothing with simple thoughts;

If the dove is to peace

as peace is to freedom

and the raven's means

meet the same end in freedom

then the raven's ill will is in vain.

For its victim will harvest salvation

even in their inevitable freedom.

Joseph R. Adomavicia

Love Unbound

Lead me to a land where love is unbound
where songs of harmony are profound.
In due time,
circumstance as cold as space
will tear apart the flesh of love,
leaving it to bleed like a sieve.
And when its cries ring out into the open,
at least then,
the vastness of its depths
would have awoken.
If love's consequence brings for the worst,
then in reciprocity above what is bleak,
it will bring the best just as well.

There must be a land
where love is unbound.

Please, Wake Up

Please,

wake up,

and when you do,

do what is good

for you and your own

within the means of the laws

meant to create order.

If you need help,

seek it.

Please,

wake up,

stop killing one another.

Killing other people fixes nothing.

It only puts death on ice skates

gliding down a slippery slope

decapitating the head of peace.

Peace stripped from the lives taken,

peace taken from the rest of the world.

Please,

wake up.

Stop killing one another.

Joseph R. Adomavicia

My Heart Was Given, My Will Was Not

See me, hear me, and feel me.

My soul lay bare—

my heart was given,

my will was not.

From your vantage point

you take advantage

of friends, money, and thoughts.

I shall not forfeit my happiness

for the sake of yours.

Can this love you claim true

be true when you bathe in sin?

Do you see, hear, and feel me

when your self-induced euphoria

numbs your perception?

See me, hear me, and feel me.

My soul lay bare—

my heart was given,

my will was not.

Lesson #76

Life can be like a field of roses:

beautiful, lush, vast, and breathtaking.

It also can be like standing

in that same field and burning to ash

from the blaze of hellish fury—

every beautiful petal,

the lushness,

the vastness,

becomes barren earth

soon to be quenched

in the waters of resolve.

And up through the ground

sprouts new life—

with or without you taking another

breath.

Joseph R. Adomavicia

Little Paper Hearts

Little paper hearts open
with faded words between the lines.
Little paper hearts close,
balled up like a writer's scrapped page.
Little paper hearts open,
crumpled and wrinkled and crinkled.
Little paper hearts open or closed
can be reshaped but shy from normal.
Little paper hearts open.
Little paper hearts close.
Love is a wager worth betting on
for, even a little paper heart
regained shape after being crumpled up
and tossed away.

River Fishing (A Haiku)

Soft river burbles

steady on a rocky bed

The fish are jumping

Joseph R. Adomavicia

A Song in the Trees (Hir a Thoddaid)

While on the front porch catching the breeze
I saw scarlet wings fly to the trees.
And from a branch its song aimed to please
this tattered heart so it beats at ease.
A cadence that soothes through many phases,
erasing the doubt of my unease.

Battle Stripes

Life flows steadily
then suddenly
it will tug, push, and pull
with the power of white-water rapids.
Keep your head above the water,
get back to shore,
and then claw back
with the power, toughness,
and conviction of a tiger
fighting for its cub's meal.
It's life or death
from first to final breath.
Scarred, tired, and tested,
you earn your battle stripes.

Joseph R. Adomavicia

Believe

May we believe in one another,

may we unite

as the name of our country insists.

To be a unit of unification living

unfettered by restrictions

within various states, cities, counties,

towns, and reservations.

A representation of people

peacefully coexisting,

withstanding difference of

opinion or belief

within the melting pot that is America.

May we act not only for ourselves,

but what is also good

for our neighbors as well.

For, if we continue to neglect acceptance,

what then,

is there to genuinely believe in?

Cerulean Wings

On Ellis Island,
Liberty Enlightens the World.
A 24-carot-gold-gilded torch is held
upward and proudly in a Patina hand.
Shall Lady Liberty's torch be doused out?
Shall her 7-pointed crown
fall to the ground
next to the broken shackles at her feet
or shall the flames in the hearts and eyes
of her people ignite the flame everlasting?
May we believe in one another,
may we unite
as the name of our country insists
because as it is, is not good enough.

Joseph R. Adomavicia

Dear Lover, Forevermore

Dear lover,

have you seen where the roses bloom?

Please, give it the thought.

For, I love you,

and if the blossoming of a rose

is love eternal

then that is how long I plan to do so.

From our first I love you,

to today's

and of course,

forevermore.

Dear lover,

have you seen where the rivers flow?

Please, give it the thought.

For, I love you,

and the connectivity of all water is

relative,

let us continue on

because that is how long I plan to do so.
From our first I love you,
to today's
and of course,
forevermore.

Dear lover,
have you noticed the sun and moon?
Please, give it the thought.
For, I love you,
and they both rise and set daily
like how we wake and fall asleep
with the joy of seeing one another.
From our first I love you,
to today's
and of course,
forevermore.

Dear lover,
have you heard of forever?

Joseph R. Adomavicia

Please, give it the thought.
For, I love you,
and if forever is the extent
of the length of our lifespans
then that is how long I plan to do so.
From our first I love you,
to today's
and of course,
forevermore.

Dear lover,
I promise,
forevermore.

Without You

Like a guitar without strings
or like a singer who has lost their voice,
without you,
I would not have the harmony
I have in my life now.

Like a captain without a ship
or like a ship lacking the sea
to set sail upon,
without you,
I would not have my bearings
set forth with confidence.

Like a river that has run dry
or an ocean without waves
without you,
I would not have the happiness
you have saved
in a heart once absent of it.

Joseph R. Adomavicia

Like a garden without soil
or like flowers without sunlight and water,
without you,
I would not have the pleasure
of having the love
we have created.
Without you I would not have.

One Thing

If I could just say
one thing.
It would be
after all this time
of all the time taken for granted
through all trials
through all tribulations
I'm so happy,
so happy,
to simply
be alive.

Dedication Page

Mom and Dad, thank you for raising me and helping me have confidence in the man I am today. Without the hard work you instilled into me over the years, I am certain I would not be the same person you know today.

Chris, you have always supported me and helped me fund my books from the beginning. You have a heart of gold and are of the most influential people in my life. No matter where life takes us, I will never forget all you have done for me, as a man, a manufacturer, and as the poet you now know.

Raymond and Billy, thank you for your unfaltering support of who I am as an individual through all highs and lows. There is something to be held sacred between siblings, may our bonds remain unbroken.

Jonathan and Dwight, although of the three of us, Dwight can longer be here I will forever cherish the moments we shared. The late-night thoughts and conversations inspire me to this very moment and always will. One day we will be reunited, but for now, I hope you look down and smile, because, without you Dwight, I quite possibly would never have put pen to paper as I have.

To all my friends, teachers, and supporters I have not mentioned, thank you. I hope my words continue to inspire and touch your hearts. At the end of the day each line I inscribe onto the page I keep you in mind and in my heart.